Patricia Salyer grew up in the Pacific Northwest, which she calls God's country. Her youth was spent on a farm, where she grew to love all animals. In the last ten years, she has devoted energy and love for rabbits. She has gotten to know bunnies such as Scamp, Sweet Pete, and Mrs. Beasley – to name a few. She plans to continue her relationship with rabbits.

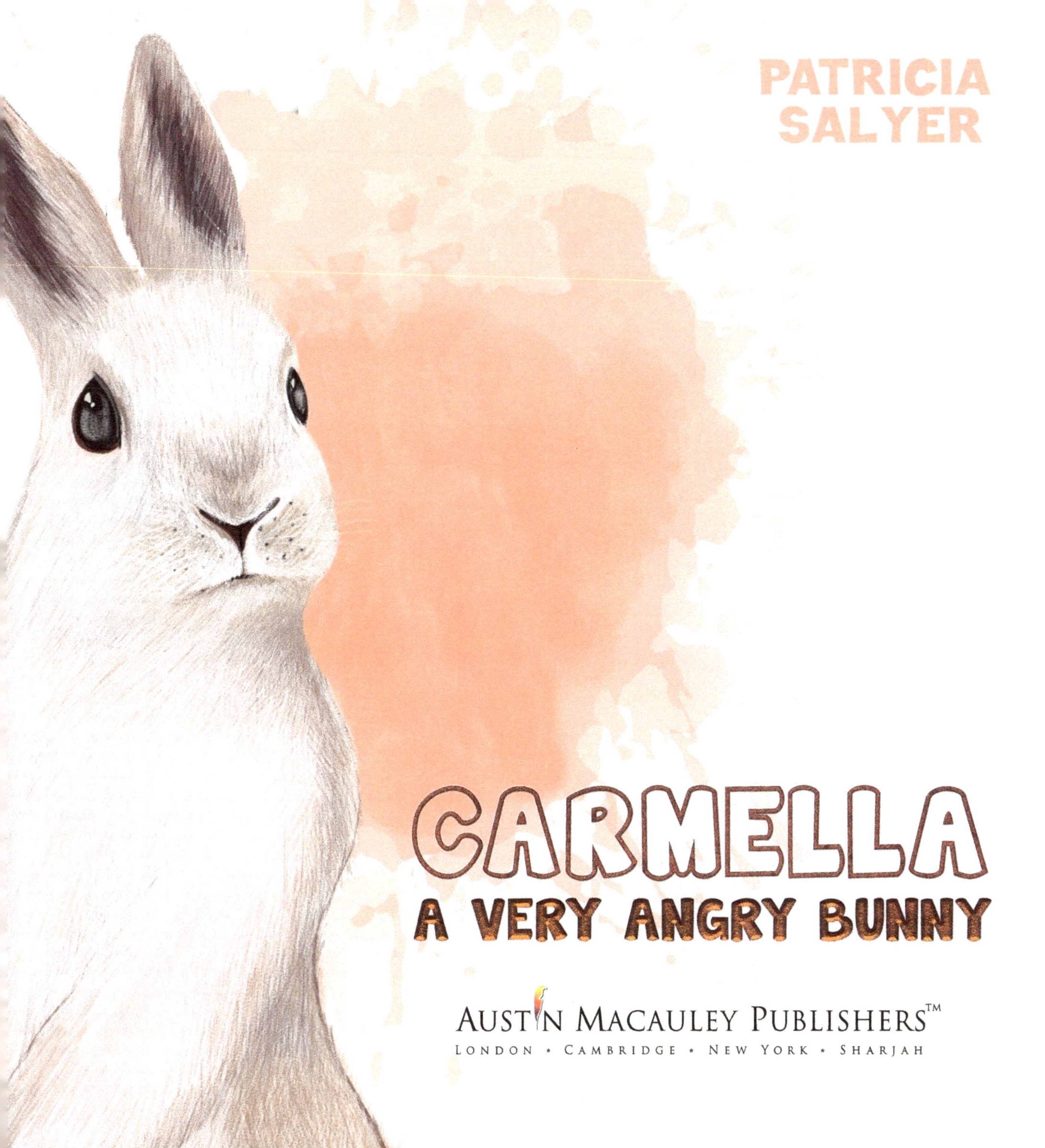
PATRICIA SALYER
CARMELLA
A VERY ANGRY BUNNY
AUSTIN MACAULEY PUBLISHERS™
LONDON • CAMBRIDGE • NEW YORK • SHARJAH

Copyright © Patricia Salyer (2020)

Ordering Information:
Quantity sales: special discounts are available on quantity purchases by corporations, associations, and others. For details, contact the publisher at the address below.

Publisher's Cataloging-in-Publication data
Salyer, Patricia
Carmella

ISBN 9781643782300 (Paperback)
ISBN 9781643782317 (Hardback)
ISBN 9781645367239 (ePub e-book)

Library of Congress Control Number: 2020911809

www.austinmacauley.com/us

First Published (2020)
Austin Macauley Publishers LLC
40 Wall Street, 28th Floor
New York, NY 10005
USA
mail-usa@austinmacauley.com
 +1 (646) 5125767

To all the bunnies.

I was not always angry. In the beginning, I was a beautiful, happy, miniature Rex bunny, white and caramel colored (thus, my name). I only weighed two pounds. My cage in the pet store was warm and cozy. I was unaware of what was ahead of me. Probably the most dangerous time of the year for bunnies - Easter!

Children whose parents know nothing about rabbits let them grab thousands of bunnies just like me. Our tiny bones - many are the size of toothpicks - break easily, including our backbones. We are tossed, squeezed, and dropped. They were trying to kill me!

When we are a few months old, our humans want to be
rid of us because we start pee-peeing around the house.
Humans do not realize that we can be potty-trained like
a cat by eight weeks old. No gritty kitty litter or wood
chips, please - we try to eat them! That is our
habit - chewing, lots of chewing, so that our teeth
do not grow too long.

The humans that originally owned me, dumped me in a cage behind a veterinarian's (vet) clinic late one night, just before a large winter storm arrived. Do you know that cold and wet weather kills bunnies? I wondered, Why have they dumped me late at night? But like other humans, they did not want someone to see them abandon their pet.

The vet came to work early before the storm arrived and rescued me. Remember, wet and cold weather kills bunnies; especially wet.

The big bunny in the sky must
have been looking out for me.

The vet's staff placed me inside a tiny flowerpot. That is when Mom came in, took one look and said, "I'll take her!" (I did not know it, but this was the beginning of a new life. Unfortunately for Mom, I was very angry and frightened. I wondered, What else
can humans do to me?)

Mom was great! She did all she could to keep me warm and safe, but she wondered why I would make small whimpering sounds. The vet said they were stress sounds. Eventually, I trusted Mom and I stopped making stress sounds - but I was still angry. I growled and leapt at everyone as though I would bite. Bunnies do growl. It sounds like a pig rooting in dirt. It was great sport, terrifying Mom's dog and cats. One growl, lunge, and bite was all it took for a 25-pound dog to go racing off!

One day, Mom felt I needed a bunny boyfriend, so she brought home Scamp, my bunny boyfriend. We loved each other at first site! Of course, Mom had both of us "fixed" (meaning that we could not have baby bunnies); which all bunny owners should do. No one wants too many baby bunnies!

After a blissful ten years together, Scamp died. I was devastated! Mom saw me curled up in a ball for several days, so she decided to rush me to the vet. The vet said I was grieving over Scamp and that she had seen rabbits grieve for over a year. Mom gave me lots of TLC (which means tender loving care) and I eventually recovered. Love you, Mom!

Now, you may think I directed my anger mainly toward bunnies and other animals; but my specialty was small children of the human kind. My earliest memories were of the little people abusing me. When Mom's grandsons; Cody, 9; and Brandon, 7, came to visit, I was "locked and loaded." During the day, I behaved myself - but at night, the anger was unleashed. For some reason, I chose the youngest grandson, Brandon, to torture.

One evening, before Brandon went to bed, he decided he wanted a banana. He sat on the sofa to eat it. Mom's daughter, Kelly, warned him he might not want to eat it around Carmella. Brandon ignored her. Then, I pounced onto his lap, ripping and clawing at his pajamas. I wanted that banana - or else!

Brandon ran screaming into the kitchen to get rid of the banana. After this, we assumed Brandon settled into his bed on the floor. I was in my enclosure.

Because Brandon and Cody were young, Mom made their beds in front of the TV, so they could watch movies while the big people slept. During the middle of the night, somehow, I managed to get out of my enclosure. I immediately set my sights on Brandon, the youngest and tenderest. Yummy!

No one will ever know what happened that night, because I did not talk, and Brandon was afraid to say why a little bunny got the better of him. Let's just say that when Mom's daughter, Kelly, got up for a glass of water, Brandon was on the sofa, and I was next to the sofa staring up at him. Kelly asked Brandon why he was on the sofa. Brandon pretended he was asleep. Cody called out, "He is afraid of the rabbit." Sorry, Brandon, the truth was told.

I was never angry with Mom; except when she was late with my banana treat and cheese crackers. Yes, you heard that right - bananas and cheese crackers! The vet was horrified! She said bunnies become addicted to bananas and cheese crackers. The only way I would go into my enclosure was for the banana and cheese crackers. Mom figured it was worth it. She was very careful to give me only a small piece of banana and two cheese crackers. I would have eaten the whole banana and the entire box of cheese crackers, which would have made me very sick.

One warm, sunny day, Mom put me in the backyard;
Happy! Happy! Joy! Joy! I hopped about munching grass
and whatever else I could get my little chiseled teeth on.
Unfortunately, Mom did not know that many plants will
not only make a bunny sick, but may kill them. I did not
know it either. After all, I'm only a little bunny.
And there it was! A huge patch of Morning Glories
covering an entire fence, in full bloom! Needless to say,
I was in the middle of the Morning Glories before you
could blink. I stuffed my little furry face.

Mom came out later and I did not respond to her voice, nor was I moving. I was also in a stiff, tight ball. Mom could immediately tell something was wrong. She rushed over and I could not look at her. My eyes were glassy and my pupils dilated. I was very ill.
Once again, there was a rush to the vet. The vet looked at me and asked, "What has she been eating?"
"Morning Glories," said Mom.

The vet said, "That explains it." She said that Morning Glories contains a liquid similar to LSD, a very powerful drug which some people like to use. The vet had to give me lots of water to wash the drug out of my body. She said I was lucky it did not kill me. She gave Mom a list of plants bunnies should never eat. For instance, here are a few: Besides Morning Glories, Azaleas, Rhododendrons, apple seeds, any bulb plants (except carrots, of course!), and much more!

Once I was well, we went home. Mom had to pull out all of her beautiful Morning Glories. She was not happy about it, but she wanted to protect me. Thanks, Mom! Mom always took me to the vet. She was good like that! She wanted me to be a healthy bunny. (She did not know what was really going on in the exam room; but I did! Those people were trying to kill me!)

Finally, bunnies do not like showing that they are in pain. It is because they could become food for many animals; for example, dogs, cats, raccoons, fox, and many others. So, one day, I could not hide my pain any longer.

I tried to hop into the living room, but I was dragging my hind leg. Mom became very upset and rushed me to the vet, again. When we walked into the lobby, we could hear the technicians screaming, "She's here."

"No, she isn't!"

"Yes, she is!"

Later, they came out to tell Mom that they were sorry
she had overheard them - but they rolled up their
sleeves and showed her all the wounds I had given
them. Mom was shocked! But I wasn't. I glared at the
technicians. When they came to the exam room, Mom
was horrified to see a picture of me on the wall! They
did not write "Carmella" on the picture. They wrote
in BIG letters:

CARMICULA

They had even colored my eyes red and showed fangs coming out of my mouth.

Please, I'm only a five and one-half pound bunny!

So - that day, the vet and Mom agreed I should be put to sleep. As she prepared me for death, she told Mom that I had tortured her technicians for more than ten years! One technician's arms and hands were covered in scars.
Before I go, I want Mom to know I love her very much, and I am sorry for any trouble I caused. I was only protecting myself from people (I thought were) trying to kill me!
Goodbye everyone. Please don't forget me!

Getting a Bunny?

1. Please, please, do research on the care and keeping of a bunny! There are magazines and books at some pet stores, the library, and even the internet. If you don't, you will have a sick, unhappy animal - or even a dead bunny. I know! I killed two beautiful bunnies because of my ignorance.

2. An exotic vet can give you information.

3. In addition, contact your local rabbit association (via the internet, magazines, phone book, or your local feed store/business which stocks feed for many kinds of animals.)

4. University vet clinics can also usually give you a wealth of information. Also, you may learn that a small bunny should drink a lot of water, daily; and that tap water makes them sick.

5. I wish you happy bunny days! They are delightful - and each has their own personality!

MOM

(Patricia Salyer, March 2018)